Robert
Miltner

hotel
utopia

Robert
Miltner

hotel utopia

Many Voices Project
Number 123

First Edition
Library of Congress Control Number: 2010933708
ISBN: 978-0-89823-255-4
MVP Number 123
Author photo by Mike Rich
Cover and interior design by Addie Borgh

The publication of *Hotel Utopia* is made possible by the generous support of the McKnight Foundation and other contributors to New Rivers Press.

For academic permission or copyright clearance please contact Frederick T. Courtright at 570-839-7477 or permdude@eclipse.net.

New Rivers Press is a nonprofit literary press associated with Minnesota State University Moorhead.

Alan Davis, Senior Editor
Suzzanne Kelley, Managing Editor
Wayne Gudmundson, Consultant
Allen Sheets, Art Director
Thom Tammaro, Poetry Editor
Kevin Carollo, MVP Poetry Coordinator
Fran Zimmerman, Business Manager

Publishing Interns:
Ryan Christiansen, Katelin Hansen, Jenny Hilleren, Samantha Jones, Tarver Mathison, Jenna Miller, Elizabeth Zirbel

Hotel Utopia Book Team:
Erica Anderson, Christine LaCoursiere, Renee LaMie, John Powers

Printed in the United States of America

New Rivers Press
c/o MSUM
1104 7th Avenue South
Moorhead, MN 56563
www.newriverspress.com

Everybody's pointing at the moon, you know, but
I'm telling you where it isn't.

**- d. a. levy
Cleveland**

Here, I would like to recount a little story so
beautiful I fear it may well be true.

**- Michel Foucault
Paris**

contents

contents

part 3

Picture the Future

for José Clemente Orozco

1.

The Conquest was a machine made of robotic horse gods and men whose indestructible armor was thunder. Monks in executioner hoods founded churches of subservience on the bones and skulls of indigenous people who were released from the navel of the world in Oaxaca and Chiapas and refused the chokehold of compromise.

2.

A man with ascendant ideas is on fire. He climbs the museum walls higher, burns his human shape into the ceiling, the cupola, the sky. Now the horses are upside down and sideways, the machines broken, the past blackened coins and ash. Change is constructed of muscle. Revolution is made from red meat.

3.

Sunlight. Art and architecture publicly owned. Fresh air. This hospice of humanity is the red of bloods mixed, the red of the sky as it ignites another dawn. The faces of the disappeared are painted on stone with water. Then they evaporate. How else would we remember them?

1

Jack, Neal, and a '49 Hudson

after a linocut by Marc Snyder

In the last year of the first half of the Modern century, Mao, the khaki emperor, was entering Beijing; Salinger was finishing *Catcher in the Rye*; Ginsberg was on the roof beginning to *Howl.* My father was walking away from the punch press at Republic Steel in Cleveland and driving off, a company man, in his first company car, to have lunch in Pittsburgh with a client where they would talk bolts and golf over cocktails and steaks. My lace-curtain, West Side Irish mother was in her eighth month, waddling with me, with my year-and-a-half-old brother in tow, catching his breath.

In Detroit, 180 miles or so north, a '49 Hudson was rolling off the automobile assembly line, its odometer at zero, an open-mouthed "O," marveling at the new highway system that Jack and Neal would drive in it, a Post-Modern Holy Trinity going coast-to-coast, over and over, because they could, because it was not about having or even about being, it was just about moving, their lust for wandering never satisfied, sighs and laughter like exhaust emitted into the air of the high-octane world into which I was being born, gasping for breath.

Red House

The door is red. You stand silent, one hand holding the other. The
house is made of stones. Your hands are vines groping. The number
of years you dwelt upon the threshold is larger than the sum of
your memories.

Your mouth, a portal. Your body, the key. The door is red. You lean on
the doorjamb, your forehead against the oak which is harder than the
choices you have been given. For years, you dreamed of windows.
The house is made of loans.

The house is made of bones. Your voice, the key to open the lock. Your
eyes are widening. The door is red. The number of times you've told
yourself lies then denied them is thicker than the door.

Your body, a door. Your life, a house. There are other houses, other
doors. You stand on the top step, fitting the door frame better than you
fit your former life. The door is red.

Your body is red. Your life is made of bones. Lean into the door, step
into yourself, through yourself, out of yourself. Your dreams are eyes.
Your eyes are windows.

The door is red and your life is a key. Open your mouth. Use your voice.

Murder of Metaphors

How the world's surface ripples with misconceptions, misreadings.

How we imagine what is real by picking a card from the hand's
spread of realities.

How analogies make abstractions dress for success, address each
audience, redress disparities.

How the difference between ignorance and prejudice is a choice of
educations: leaving the classroom, its books stacked on the desk, or
entering the father's room, its flag and willow switch in the corner.

How weight sits lightest on those who won't listen.

How we find ourselves caught in a run of clubs or situated among
perspectives, like the seven surrounded by diamonds.

How where we stand dictates the objects we hold in our hands:
guns or words.

White Hotel

They wore white linen suits.

They laughed like water in a mountain stream.

They ate veal in what used to be a medieval monastery, unaware of how the vaulted ceilings and arched windows absorbed all conversation.

They found themselves astounded to find it took the peasants three generations to build the abbey.

They discussed how the monks used to sing Alleluias in this very room.

They shook their heads upon learning novices were required to sleep on rope beds in unadorned cells.

They read in their brochures that actual historical figures once walked these same streets.

They lifted their glasses, the white wine clear as spring water.

They liked the way the table candles lighted their faces.

Box of Light

Joseph Cornell lived on Utopia Parkway. Walking the sidewalk, he
filled his pockets with recyclable oddities and fragments of moonlight.
Arriving home, he affixed them lovingly into little wooden boxes: rooms
of their own poetics.

We're on our way to the Hotel Utopia. Our socialist and anarchist
friends sleep there like found art in the small rooms with the inclusive
balconies. They rent for a sonnet when breathing and politics are twins.
Just past the lobby is Lefty's Bar & Grill. We drink to labor and art, talk
louder than the atomic jukebox. Porters on draft and stout in the cooler
are what the struggle tastes like.

After the revolution, stop by. We'll raise our glasses and sing along with
Woody Guthrie or the Sierra Leone Refugee All Stars. The rooms still
use metal keys that sleep in the hammock of a pocket and parking is free.
How many stars, you ask? We're all stars at the Hotel Utopia.

Shadow

What if a man stands directly under the sun? What if the sun is a genre? OK, make the man stand under a genre. Call it noon. His shadow leaks from his shoes. His shadow calls for his brother, the night. What if his shadow was a crow?

Alone, he holds the crow down on the sidewalk. In this asymmetrical power relationship, he deems himself in control, calm as a comma. He stands within the boundary of a sentence. Period.

OK, make the genre stand under the man. When the sun rises in his prose, it casts a long black poem. What if it looked like a bat in a box? A crow in a used car? Make it a stolen car, right there, where the shadow used to be. Right there, under his shoes.

Refugees

after a painting by Tamara de Lempicka

Framed by the silver train window are a woman and her daughter. The child leans her head on her mother's shoulder; the mother's arm, a shawl holding her daughter. Each wears a coat the gray of a sky about to storm.

Their eyes are black stones from a country road. Home is back down the track. What's next is as uncertain as the outcome of a civil war, as shocking as watching the neighbors being shot.

Mother and daughter carry bundled tablecloths colorful as a sunrise igniting the sky. They hold a clutch of belongings, their hope useless as a pocket full of foreign coins.

For the moment, each is thankful for the simple grace of sitting. Tonight they know where sleep will carry their bodies. They don't know what country their bones will wake in.

Uninhabited World

Our village was all the world we needed. We bred red birds until we could afford babies. At night our bodies were string beans in a box. You worked so hard your nails cracked while my hands bled from the sharp stones, relics I dug from the dirt so we could sow seed in the fields. I set down my hoe when the government forces trampled the oats and planted landmines to explode under the insurgents' feet.

While they rounded up goats, ducks, and the other young men, we slipped through shadows from our home to a farm shed at the village edge. Do you remember how we awoke to the patch of blue sky in the roof? To the yellow birds nesting in the eaves? To the kick of army boots and gun butts? We looked like sardines removed from the can. At the refugee camp we were peapods and sheep, stripped and shorn.

Each morning I see laden carts pushed toward the open pit over the small hill beyond which the wind goes to die. Last month I aged a thousand years, this week another hundred more. Salt will soon settle on my shadow, my bones covered in lime. I dream my body is a white bird that flies around this beating world. You'll know it's me, floating like a kite, a skeleton holding an unsigned poem.

How to Draw a Horse

after an intaglio print by Marc Snyder

Begin with a pyramid. With an Egyptian riding a horse across the
sandy expanse, planning to have his cats and liver accompany him to
the afterlife, a place where honey lasts forever.

After the Israelites leave, the British will arrive, pockets stuffed with
guns and laws. They'll fill the coal cars with pirated mummies, toss
them into the locomotive's fire, fuel for the colonial train.

But today the Egyptian basks in the sun like a sphinx, head held high,
centered in a momentary universe. A cloud covers the sun like an eye
patch, then passes, leaving only a horse.

Café La Habana, Mexico City

No, we didn't want café americano. We were hungry and wanted *pan dulce* to eat on the run. But the menu was full of meals and plates, sit and stay. Over the clutter of dishes and cutlery we heard the horns and congas of salsa music. The espresso was weak and had coarse coffee grounds as gritty as beach sand. Our guidebook explained how Fidel ate here regularly while he was exiled and planning his return trip on the old boat Granma to launch the revolution. We saw him, a cigar in his mouth, at various tables, then he sat down with us. We must all sacrifice for the revolution, no? he asked. He patted our shoulders then returned to his table, his maps, his plans, his place in history. We paid our bill and left a tip worthy of a better world. Stepping out of the café, we wanted the underground rail, but found ourselves among the Agricultural Workers Syndicate, mostly indigenous people with noses sharp as shovels, on their way to a political rally. When we came to the next block, we turned left.

Blue House

She was broken. Her piñata had spilled its candy to the floor. She wanted to be whole.

He was larger than life, complete of himself. He broke into her life, stole her solitude.

Her upper body required it always be held in plaster's hand. She wanted to be held in a wooden frame.

His energy was an enormous room where clocks broke and calendars withered and fell to the floor.

She was a bed with a looking glass on the ceiling. Art was her mirror.

He was every face in the land since before the corn mothers left, every face since the revolution.

The light from within her illuminated every canvas she entered. One was coyote, one was monkey. One was hammer, one was scythe. One was clock, one was not.

His canvas was history. He was stele, a stone wall. He painted murals with images that left the margins and took on lives of their own, telling their stories.

She was ceramic figure, fired clay, cracked vase, blue house. She was the personal pain of the body, the damaged spine.

He was the body crushed by poverty and domination, the burdened back, shackle and brand. He was adobe wall.

She painted herself as far as the frame. She was art's mirror.

He was whole. His piñata was filled with salt. He wanted to be broken.

Safety Limits

Ice forms first near the shore, extending out toward the middle where it meets, smooth as chrome. Careful, the parents call out to their children, what looks solid could be as thin as a razor blade; you could fall like a coin into an arcade game. But the children's eyes are wide as the sky.

Skates on, the kids glide across the glazed center. Watch out, the parents warn, the border between what's solid and what's air is a wound, a suture, a scar. The boys and girls open their coats like sails on boats, and the wind blows them like dead leaves into the distance.

Blue, the curtain draped and hanging where the sky and the lake converge; white, the northern sky offering no parting, no stage exit. Beware, the parents say, you can never catch that horizon you are chasing. But the kids are picking up speed, lifting, rising like kites.

Blockheads, Bastards

1.

Just two people simultaneous in their actions, irresponsible as teens sneaking out at midnight to meet at the park, their eyes vivid as knives, bodies hot as lighters. Maybe responsibility, that odd man out, left somewhere around the third round of drinks when they shifted from sweet California white to vulgar Spanish red.

2.

Did Lady Poetry want to tame Mister Prose? Or did he, if only for an instant, change from water to wine?

Fusion, each thought.

Blur, she whispered.

Impure, he pawed.

Hyphenate, they moaned.

Baby, each said.

3.

Caliban stands in his crib, stuck in his square, a crow cawing for attention. All that glitters outside his cell will be pulled in through the bars after he learns to bend them. Ask him which wine he wants, the red or the white. Rosé, he'll reply, his tongue a sharply honed blade, his words bright as butane flames.

Speechless

You are a disordered coat in search of a suitable body. Your cuffs frayed, your socks chewed at the heel by shoes that leak like old boats stressed at the seams from too many nights rowed hard against the tide, your whole ensemble as much a lie as the memories of dogs you once owned that neither listened nor heeled.

Cars hiss by on rainy streets, headlights glaze the pavement, illuminating the revelations taunting you from the next corner or down another alley.

You hurry to meet the fragments of found art awaiting you at the only coffee shop still open where neon, spilled for hours on the laminated counter top, sinks into the paled skin of meaning's vague face that stares unblinkingly at you, silent as a mummy, your name lying dumb on its tongue.

Accident

Gray was the truck cab, black its body. Yellow the taxi in front, red the surround of the traffic signal.

The tomato-faced driver eyed his watch, behind schedule with green dreams of money and lust's blue fantasies. For him, the signal was still a singing canary.

For the man and woman, the light had changed. Neither could stop thinking about what he had said to her that morning.

Their fingers brushed. She took his hand in the rain at the crosswalk at that hour. The truck was blacktop, macadam, raven, crow.

Then the umbrella slipped from her grip. Then her face was waxen in the green light, his burnt umber turning raw sienna.

Silver from the street lamps splayed on the pavement. Red from the traffic light ran across the wet asphalt.

House Noises at Night

How does the foundation sound as it settles?

No kiss in the tongue and groove, no wrath as plaster separates from
lathe, and here, under these sills, hairline cracks pretend to be fault lines,
portending the eventual entry of insect, water, rodent, cold.

How cold, how dark is silence?

Plumbing lines, sink drains, vent stacks, cold water feeds slowly corrode
closed like overindulged arteries: highways for centipedes and other
drivers in the dark. How deep the insects burrow, the piles of sawdust
forming small pyramids.

How ragged is anger?

With the first disappointment, understanding. With the second, forgiveness.
With the third, irritation like a burr in the sock, no sidestepping. With the
fourth or four hundredth, words load like dumdum bullets.

How true is the algebra of emptiness?

Doors awkward as first kisses stick at the jamb, dead bolts and strike plates
misalign, the night air burgles under the door and over the threshold, what
swings squeaks: the divorce of proper closure.

2

American Spleen

Calm down, the deceptive husband tells the jealous wife, you're just being
hysterical — call your doctor and have him prescribe a sedative. When he
hands her the cell phone, her loose hand tightens into a fist. She aims for his
head. After Baudelaire, why not vent a little spleen?

Doctors say we can do splendidly without the spleen, lumping it in with the
appendix, tonsils, toes, an ear or eye. Yet perform a splenectomy to remove
it and then what? Drown our sorrows as well as our livers?

Without spleen, there'd be no kidding, no satire, no poking us in the ribs
and looking in the mirror. Instead of Jonathan Swift or Kurt Vonnegut,
we'd be left with Danielle Steele or Doctor Phil. Instead of books, we'd be
left with only the TV. Who wouldn't rather be drugged?

The Arts

for Gil Scott-Heron

The arts will not be on the test.

Math will be on the test because it shows how to count the numbers
of homeless people the TV won't show, helps calibrate how to pepper
specks of depleted uranium across whatever land is being bombed, how
to estimate the amount of time needed to react to the media prompt and
not be the prompt itself.

The arts will not be on the test.

Science will be on the test because engineering builds equivocations
effective enough to justify hypocrisy; physics enables occupation to be
set in motion without friction; and astronomy helps the poor search the
sky instead of their empty plates.

The arts will not be on the test.

A poem has no square root; a song has no chemical compound; a guitar
solo will not fit on a bell curve; a dance cannot be reduced to a lowest
common denominator; an actor resists dissection, fights being pinned
down on cotton; a story has no mean, no mode, no medium.

The arts will not be on the test.

There will be no matching columns on truth and beauty, no multiple
choice selections on content, no fill-in on form, no short answer on craft,
no comprehension questions on aesthetics, no essay on the nation's soul.
No, none of the above.

The arts will not be on the test.

Stairway to Heaven

The Ursuline nuns used to tell us grade-school kids, it always rains on
Good Friday. But when we looked out the window the skies were blue as
colored Easter eggs and the trees were flowering bright as fireworks.

That's how it is when reason's path disappears in the dark woods: the
faithful light their way with faith. Like a drowning man clutching a flimsy
airplane seat, what else is there to hold on to? What's gospel to some seems
to others more like myth, fable, tall-tale, some talk-the-child-to-sleep story.

Like the one about the man who by his own hand throws the money-
lenders out of the temple. Who turns bones into soup for the poor. Then
gets nailed to a cross between those two thieves, the Republicans on the
right, the Democrats on the left.

The Uprising

after a painting by Honoré Daumier

When pent-up frustration, choked down like bad meat, suddenly erupts, people take to the streets. A river of revolution courses through the arteries to the city's center heart where the government offices and banks form a square. Fists clenched, arms raised, citizens rally and rail, chant and curse, their lungs the bellows for the fires of insurrection. When rage has burned to embers, their mouths dry and throats raw, they'll retreat to kitchens, porches, or bars, talk ebulliently and drink riotously, before dropping into their beds like spent bullets.

Black House

We can imagine our own death. Jumping off a bridge, rushing in front of a speeding truck, or even igniting ourselves as a noble protest against some ignoble cause. We can, and we do. But we cannot dream about actually dying.

At the moment just before the boat overturns, before the mob attacks, before the firing squad squeezes the triggers, we wake up with our heart pounding, our throat so dry that we don't dare swallow for fear our esophagus will shatter, a sound like windows being blown out from a drive-by shooting.

If we dream in color, we can see the blood, red as when we force our eyes shut against the setting sun, though we know that it's no more real than an actor's prop, a magician's trick, a sideshow gimmick.

In the morning we shower, our heads under the faucet with its noose of water, and we remember residual images from our dream arrayed like still shots from a movie trailer. Eyes closed, we don't see the swirl of red spinning clockwise down the drain.

Extreme Junction

So what if life opens like a morning, a minute, or a month?

Disregard the afternoon's slow revels, or how soon the day rescinds.
When the curtain falls, the theater exhales its darkness.

The growing shadows of ghosts haunt sleep. If sleep comes at all.

When dusk arrives like drawn shades, people appeal to the nearest priest
for a stand-by flight to the afterlife. Tighter than coffins or canning jars
they screw their eyes.

The light finally arrives like rapture and claims its seat in the balcony,
while the afterlight ruptures evening's dark box.

So what if death closes like a mummy, a moth, or a mouth?

Hope

Desperate acts create their own vocabulary. So when I drove my ailing father-in-law to the cancer clinic in Buffalo, he called it *worth a try*. He carried his own x-rays in a large envelope as if they were his passport to another country.

While he sat up on the examination table, the doctor silently moved the x-rays of the cancerous esophagus first one way, then another, tapping them occasionally with his finger, as if they were tarot cards waiting to be turned over. My father-in-law's future seemed as exposed as his own uncovered back, half-gloved in a flimsy blue hospital gown.

After we left the clinic, we stopped a few blocks away at a local bar, nursing Iron City drafts and avoiding eye contact. We watched a ball game on a boxy TV in the dark, narrow bar, hoping someone would win that day.

The sun was setting as we drove out of the city. The car's headlights stretching out ahead on the dusking road, searching weakly for what was waiting in the dark. My father-in-law called it *what's left*. He called it *what's next*.

The Utter Beauty of Water

after a kimono painting by Itchiku Kubota

At dawn I awoke and looked out the seaside window. A horizon line was
drawn by a ruler of sea and sky. What light there was registered in the
upper portion of my vision.

But I was attracted to the lower region, to the bay with its gray
spaces where what's shallow shows, the green-blue troughs, the
waves white-capping against the distant space.

Drawn to the water, I swam to a sandbar where my feet touched
bottom. How odd it felt to stand, bouncing on my toes against the
swirl of eddies, the pull of the salt current.

Soon I tired of that. Then felt a shift. My cottage was a cage where
crickets sang. My world was bigger than my window. Spellbound,
I floated into the red-orange rays of the setting sun, toward an
uncertain joy.

In the Orchard, 1891

after a painting by Edmund Charles Tarbell

What a time we had that afternoon: four wooden chairs and a table
carried outside and set up under dappled shade. Around us, the trees
were filled with apples and pears, thrushes and wrens. Everything was
a figure in a bright landscape.

The women wore their dresses long with boots laced high. Men
picnicked in straw hats, ties, striped coats, and moustaches. It was an
era of redheads and brunettes, pomade and parted-down-the-center hair.
A world filled with meaningful looks, gestures. A wistfulness of wrists,
an erotics of necks.

One woman stood, a hand rolled in her apron, the other on her hip. She
shifted her weight imperceptibly and a century changed: from earth
tones and pastels, lavender and sienna, to the black and white of zinc
photographs, as monochromatic as the motor-sound heard coming
down the road, spooking the horses which leaped the fence, leaving
a rough tear across the known canvas.

Birth of the Cool

after an action painting by Jackson Pollock

A world fell on its side in 1950. Ming toppled by Mao. Teal paint splattered on the shingle. Dramatic sweeping gestures. Nuclear granaries spinning out electricity and cancer. Protons and neutrons, Ozzie and Harriet, Dole and Dulles, black and white giving way to Technicolor. Highways scarred the American landscape like a holiday ham, decorated the cloverleaf interchanges like pineapple slices. Crazy form, that's what Kerouac called it. Snow and mustard spilled on the roadside picnic tables. Miles Davis moving beyond chords to flocks of solo notes and crows. And miles of highways bled the cities out to the cul-de-sac suburbs, new kinds of expansive fields. Kinsey moving away from penetration and procreation to multiple orgasms. Multiple partners. Chaos leading to new rhythms and re-order. Snow and blood on the parking lot blacktop. The fifth element. The fourth side of the canvas. The window on the floor was a reflecting pool, the subconscious expressing emotion, a TV for a space man, a gravestone fallen on its side.

Rock the Boat

I dock and meet the woman from Islaroja. We sit at her kitchen table
drinking red wine and eating peppermint ice cream. Our tongues burn.

Desire is our boat. All night we row toward the receding shore. Our
clothes are soaked and sticking to our skin. Rain gathers in our mouths.

Dawn, and the rowboat wrecks on the coast. An ibis steps out from
behind the calla lilies. Moths open and close their wings like pliers.
We are beyond repair.

Bones

Ropes to boats, stairs to airplanes, the dirigible drops its ballast, fires
up the burners, rises. *Get down!* barks the owner to the dog. Water bowl
turned over. Fix the dog to calm it down and all the dog will want to do
is eat.

Turned over to the county kennel for adoption, no ropes to walk these
dogs, no door to bark by. Lost dogs often languish in cinderblock
buildings before being put down. Even their loss won't lift. Degrees of
compassion are comparable to stairs or stars, ocean liners or rowboats.

At the hot air balloon show, one figure was a doghouse, one a hot dog,
one a dog. The ropes loosened, the balloon dog started to float away.
One step beyond that rope, and it would have known more than one
home. Would have gone where the bone is buried or the boat is adrift.

Water Margin Bandits

after a scroll painting by Matsumura Goshun

The merchants who ply this river's trade route, bent over to count coins, see neither scenery nor us. Soon they will stop, tie up at the riverbank, nap when sleep lies on them heavy as moneybags.

Sudden as a thunderstorm, we will wake them, tie them to a tree with the rope from their anchor. Our hands wrapped around their bags of brass and silver, we'll take all the rice wine we find. Then steal their boat.

When the last bottle of wine is as empty as our threats, we will wear the merchants' coin sacks like hats. Now we are pirates! we will laugh, drunkenly letting the current carry us like good investments.

Greed

Who can resist it, lying there in the mouth, tasting like liqueur distilled from stolen candy?

You know its scent, ripe apples taken from the neighbor's yard then eaten in the dark. Your hunger for it is the insatiable appetite you save for the avaricious flesh of your lover.

Feel it, sleek as a snake's skin, slick as a tongue, hot as a loaded gun.

Remember the red crayon your hand pinched from the box and pocketed so you wouldn't have to share it with the other kids? The desire, the gluttony for color?

Greed is lean as a skeleton's shadow and will change its shape to meet your needs.

Go on, it whispers in your ear, No one is looking.

Feast Day in the Colonies

Our three-legged pig has been run over by a hay cart. I use my
grandfather's cleaver to cut the meat from the bone. Even the gristle
and fat go into the great iron pot. The sizzle is like the sound of the
locusts we eat. The dried vegetables we add look like pieces of shed skin.
Gravy is the day's gift. While we gnarled four squat in dappled shade,
the old woman sings, her voice raspy as an empty bag. The one-eared
boy watches from a distance, his eyes glistening like grease.

As Filigree

All favoritism involves a degree of value above zero. As cars rust badly in the Midwest: doors, wheel wells, exhaust.

All-in-favor is arriving lately, disembarking shortly. As corn, also in the Midwest.

Humor in the classroom is what passes for currency. As stocking-stuffer.

The long strings of nepotism are traditional, historical. As filigree of family.

Pass-the-buck is a parlor game, a kitchen-table board game, a shameless in-bed game. As naughty-lite, as erotic.

Let pass the check-out time: resist, restructure, realize. Sign the guest register. As it was in the beginning.

Empire is on the mend. Hope you enjoy the Holy day. As holiday.

Card Trick

All reward is virtued. Each episode is a celebration.

The mouse feeds on the hawk. An orphan's shadow rises.

All the children hum Vivaldi, sit quietly so their teachers can properly instruct, get good grades, abandon arcade games.

The mailbox is empty. Lies are on the wing.

The well is contaminated with PCB's and other toxic acronyms. The basement is full of water. A baby floats like a drowned bird on the waterbed again.

All our flights get edited, our itineraries reviewed.

Each bird is another puzzle piece, each child is a part of the cover design.

The crow flies sideways. Phones won't ring.

No one at the door. Nothing up my sleeve.

Pick a card, any card. Aces and eights. The three of Birds.

Watch my hands. *Watch my hands.*

Over the Border

The dark-eyed young woman behind what serves as a bar.

The clay cup into which she pours tequila. How many fingers? *Dos.*

The distance between you and the greasy man slouching next to you.
He also watches the young woman.

The keen edge of your jealousy.

The knife you keep hidden in your boot.

The small hole poked between his ribs where his life leaks out onto the
floor, slowly, pooling.

The distance between you and the dark-eyed young woman.

The time you have left before the authorities arrive.

The sound her tears make on the floor, rain after lightning.

The distance between you and the border, that scar between countries.

The laugh you throw as you leave. How many fingers now? *Uno.*

Street, City, State, Zip

Attracted to the light reflecting from glassine packages, a child releases his hold on his mother's hand, becomes adrift, drifting, caught in the instantaneous current of the crowd and swept away.

The authorities are summoned, a search commences, a van full of reporters arrives, the camera's lights are beamed on the empty space. But where has the child gone?

Who's moving under the pile of blankets and newspapers in a doorway down the alley there, as the city, an unwrapped gift, wakens to another day of white skies and blue winds?

Under a new moon, the border is breached. A shadow slips from shrub to rock to tree trunk. A voice we deny, as we fall into the canyons of sleep, reveals an image of the horizon as two arms, open, embracing the emptiness.

Late Capitalism

after a print by Julie Friedman

Time is a pliers pressing night into morning. Open and empty, it looks
like a phone, a parenthesis.

Phone lines and power lines form the net holding the industrial dawn
as it burns the gray wood of the closed factory red as a country barn.

A hundred men once worked under this corrugated metal roof, running
machines that made copper pipe.

As the night shift arrived, the firehouse next door slept uneasily,
surrounded by a neighborhood constructed of cheap lumber dried to
tinder, where hopeless exhaustion ignites hope chests with
broken hinges.

The sky is smoke, dust, heat, a fogged mirror after a muggy
summer storm.

Water streaked on the sides of buildings looks like the kind of lines
fingers make: a world is revealed beyond, behind, like unearthing by
hand a lost crypt or buried city.

A dog barks as if it hears horses that used to pull the fire wagon here,
wheels as round as rain barrels, red as poppies under the blue-white
gas lights.

The power generator's decibel hum sounds like a dial tone from the past.
It rings but no one answers.

3

Three Dog Night

Mongrel

Of course the new hybrid cars will run better: mixed, fusioned,
jammed and jambalaya-ed like that, the richer, tastier, sweeter the
treat becomes. I tell you, purebred is dead and in-between is in. Binaries
create parentheses, opening space for impossible possibilities. Think
Tex-Mex, think Bollywood. Boundaries are coming down everywhere
despite the sales of invisible fences, and all the steak bones are rolling
to my bowl. Soon we'll all be one in the urban hood, the global market.
Think Jackalope, think one giant sperm-donors' club of random,
interchangeable canines. Next time you call one of us in to eat, we'll
all come running.

Pedigree

The She wants me fixed but the He says, What are you, nuts? This is
a cash-bitch; we'll breed her, sell the puppies, and take a cruise in the
Bahamas.

Last year I did eleven shows and brought home ten ribbons — you just
wait until next year! I am a primary color, a whole note, a major key. My
nickname is Purity. I live in the suburbs. The air conditioning is nice. I
don't do much except eat and get groomed. I look so fabulous the She
takes me to the mall. Someday — you'll see — I'll star in the remake of
Lady and the Tramp. Which one will I be? Oh, you silly boy, don't doubt
me — the He has hired an agent who is to call any day. We sleep with
our cell phones.

Stray

Since I'm no alpha, I don't lead. Nixed, I'm no beta who fawns and
follows. I'm lobo, loco, a loco-motive that's jumped the track. Before, I
was oppressed—locked in a lousy one-bedroom apartment while my owner
worked late. All I could think about was not peeing or getting smacked.

So that day at the park when my owner turned to ogle a wailing baby, I was
gone, I was Gandhi, I was liberated! Boundaries aren't where I stop, they're
where my presencing begins. Call me X-marks-the-spot, or better still,
X-marks-what-used-to-be-Spot's spot.

A System of Familiar Philosophy

after a print by Wendy Collin Sorin

1.

Go to hell or Connaught, Cromwell told them, pointing a loaded
blunderbuss. Step dancing at checkpoints. Boots searched, everyone
out of the car, lined along the lane, sucked like breath into the mouth of
Maze Prison. It feels like someone's brother was stolen or kidnapped,
only not by fairies or Tinkers. The Brits who man the corner can't frisk
emails; using keyboards or cell phone texts, hands do the talking.
Partition speaks as loud as car bombs. Uilleann pipes accompany the
silence after the keening is over.

2.

Go to Derry, go to Dublin. The common song is the long hand
reaching, claiming kin. The talk is the same on both sides of the
border, the vowels sound rounder here, flatter there, while the R's
trill about the same. Each thinks the other's words sound soft as butter,
gentle as linen left long in soft mist. A divided island can never
be whole, never be one mouth making an "O" into a song. Buried in
the peat bog, under the cut-stone cross, is the same set of chromosomes,
two poor brothers sharing a bed.

The John Reed Book Club

Reed and I are passing Zapata his pistolas, Guevara his cigar, Trotsky his typewriter.

They can't do this revolution without us, gringo, Reed says.

I say, but what about the hungry hundreds of thousands waiting for the direction a certain hand will point them?

Paper, he says. Write about it.

As soon as the light turns red I run across the street to Railway Stationary. On aisle seventeen I find notebooks and lead pencils. But the checkout lines are long with people buying staples. Everything is two-for-one. Nothing is moving. Hurry, I say, the revolution is starting.

Reed sticks his head through the doorway and shouts, consumers of the world unite!

Everyone opens their cell phones to text the world.

I walk out the door and join The Marxists on the band bus. We're done shopping. I load my lead pencil into a rifle. It's going to be a long tour.

Burn after Reading

Read the poem to find out who the author is.

Why do you think the poet uses imagery?

Is the poet being literal or figurative when he talks about "rights"?

Is the poet over-generalizing when he says "all television is propaganda"?

Can one "harbor a terrorist" without a boat?

Does "conspiracy" mean more than "breathing together"?

What is a "free speech zone"? Is there one in your town?

What are the "problems" listed here?

What is revealed by the poet's library records?

How long can the author be held without trial?

Write the name of a person you suspect of being jealous of your freedoms.

Working with a partner, write an ending to the poem.

The Disappeared

Waiters will begin removing your drinks momentarily. You might want to call the people whom you were supposed to meet. We will start dismissing from the back first. They say it is quite different from this across the street at our competitor's, but I don't really know.

I can't think of anyone who wants to hold your head in her hands.

It really doesn't matter if you cooperate or not. Please follow the recommended procedure. Deviations will not be deemed suitable under any circumstances. Only so many of you have been allotted space.

Missing actually helps to define what *remaining* means.

Don't panic should you smell anything unusual. The reason for the cancellation is at present unknown, remains hidden. It is just one of the waiters or several of the busboys that you hear talking sotto voce like that. In third world countries we hear this is part of the regular routine.

You might want to take your coat with you just in case.

Itinerary

Today we are going to see the Paleolithic mounds.

Tomorrow we visit the famous battle site.

Yesterday we took the ferry to the peninsula.

Be sure to be on time for the tour bus.

Over there is a quaint little shop.

The local folk seem so polite here.

Some of their words sound like coins jangling in pockets.

They look a lot like you, wear almost the same clothes.

They won't speak English except to tell you the price.

None of them will look you in the mouth.

Many of them talk with their hands.

Some of the young mothers breastfeed babies in church.

The narrow roads wind and curve back to where they started.

The exchange rate will confuse you — twenty-seven of the silver ones with wings make a dollar.

You should be able to figure out how much this country is costing you.

It can mean *thank you* when they say that.

Algerian Memorandum: Dien Bien Phu Redux

How can we ever forget how hilarious it was? The scene in the movie (you know the one) where Laurel and Hardy join the Foreign Legion and we watch the French Lieutenant walk, with his moustache and swagger, down the line of conscripts and misfits, shouting, I need two volunteers to step forward! But everyone else takes a step back, leaving our two Beau Hunks (Hardy and Laurel) as exposed as the failures in Indochine. Funny as hell.

So Stan and Ollie and the rest of the boys, marching to Édith Piaf's torch song "No, I Regret Nothing" (in French of course), are shipped off to Algeria, where it is 1946, and our comic duo leads the raids in the Aurés Mountain villages of Kherrata and Sétif where they fire at will on the uncivilized hoards of women, children, the elderly. Bloody good fun. (Remember the dismemberments? The torture? The castrations?) God, weren't we crazy? We laughed till we had tears in our eyes. We laughed so hard we cried.

August Dogs

It was a hot and cranky day. Wally was complaining to his neighbor Jack that Jack's tree — the new one Jack got from K-Mart and just planted, a red maple — was casting shade on Wally's just-chemmed lawn.

Jack just walked away. So Wally got out a can of gasoline from his garage, doused the tree, and flicked a Bic lighter. The tree burst into bright flames. Neighborhood kids gathered, a holiday look on their faces.

Jack came out of his house with a shiny new firearm and aimed it at Wally, firing point blank with live ammo. Neighborhood kids gathered, a documentary look on their faces.

The police came. The EMS unit came. A fire truck came. Wally left with the EMS unit. Jack left with the police. The fire truck left with the neighborhood kids running behind like noisy tin cans tied to a bumper, their faces glowing like TV screens with the imprint of fresh news.

You Know What They Say about Pears

<hr>

Frumpy, heavy-hipped, green with envy of apples, the pears wear babushkas and pull carts filled with celery and cabbage out past West 88th and Detroit. Grainy sweet like candy eaten at the beach, freckled in or out of the sun, a pear is the younger child all brothers and sisters watch out for but never want to play with. The sad pears — Bartlett and Bosc, Seckel and d'Anjou — cry themselves to sleep after looking in the mirror. Everyone sees them as teardrops, as tongueless bells unable to celebrate, or as quotation marks with nothing to say. In their dreams, they run away to Hollywood and become avocados.

Schism

He wore his skin like a shell. He kept another skin inside, the difference between bark and bite, smoke and fire. He knew the questions long after the answers.

Reaching down into his throat, he pulled himself inside out, sock-like, sack-like, right in the street, his internal works as exposed as a busted watch.

Many ran away in fear, thinking him an alien. Others called for seizure, locking him up as a lunatic. A few embraced him, calling him Messiah. They ran him for public office. They ran him out of town.

Crossfire

after a painting by Pablo Picasso

Jesus decides he's been hanging around long enough, so he gets down off the cross. He finds Mary Magdalene and they go see Mary Madonna. Holding out his nail-holed hands, Jesus demands, Give us the baby.

Mary Madonna gathers the new babe in the folds of her blue robe. Her dread of being abandoned is larger than her anxiety of having to be her own comfort. She wants this baby to live long enough to care for her when she is old. All the public life gave Jesus was death.

Mary Magdalene reeks of drama queen and Jesus smells of myrrh and gall. The baby holds a scent of breast milk, oil paint. He will remain water and not turn to wine, Mary Madonna decrees. Let the world have its thieves and martyrs, its politics and game shows — my baby is private issue.

Mary Madonna swaddles her silence and Mary Magdalene holds the spikes. Jesus grasps a stone. Somewhere in the city, in a boardroom where the real decisions are made, Pilate is washing his hands.

Nostalgia

Our mad Uncle used to scare the neighborhood kids who'd gather in
the yard. Grabbing them by the shoulders in that crazed stare of his,
the slobbery chin. He'd whisper in their ears, *remember*, the sound like a
locomotive in a tunnel, growing louder.

So we called him Reptile Man, Horse-Face, Side Show Geek, Whack-Job,
though we knew he was no more than an ass with a fake unicorn horn,
some sane person impersonator.

When Father finally locked him away in the attic, Uncle threw, from
the tiny window in the cupola, bits of paper that read, *forget me.* They
fluttered to the ground like the feathers of exploded birds or the ashes
of burnt martyrs.

We gathered them, piling them in a corner of the old barn, a nest of
scraps, a paper igloo, scurrying in and out like lost mice, like blind
orphans. The days were growing shorter. We could feel the cold pull
of credulity in the air, as if a train had just rushed past. *Uncle,* we
said, surrendering.

Border, Scar

Generals and Presidents draw lines with swords and pens, leaving marks across the rocks, then down into and back out of the arroyo. Knives up their sleeves, they pat each other on the back, pose for photographs with smiles white as bleached bones.

In such and such a year some general or another moved the demarcation line from that river to this one. Borders migrate through treaty, appropriation, theft, war, illusion, mirage, or public relations.

As people sleep, a border moves over them like a blanket, a shadow, a sandstorm, so they awaken to passports and checkpoints. The money is a different color, the courts conducted in an unknown language. But flags still fly to blindfold them, and Coca-Cola and ATMs are always available.

So they adapt to the new land and vote religiously for privilege, torture, and empire. So they thump tables and march in the streets, ignored by the throngs on the sidewalks who've been conditioned to fear them. So they arm themselves, load guns with the words *no more*, call themselves Sinn Fein, Shining Path, Lakota, Independentistas.

Like all refugees and displaced people, they want land, identity, self-determination, peace, and a language to express it in before the words dry to the paper of useless land deeds in their mouths. Before blood spreads like a diaspora across the rocks.

Suitcase Full of Miracles

On her pilgrimage to Mexico she visits the sacred places of her faith,
glass houses holding images of the Virgin. In Café La Habana, she sits at
a table where Fidel and Raul could watch the doors, their backs against
the wall, cigars in their holsters. After leaving Frida Kahlo's Blue House,
she can't get through the rain and mosquitoes to Trotsky's. Soaking in
the hot-springs where Zapata bathed before he was killed, she loses her
head. Closing her eyes, she feels moustaches like huge moths against her
face. She wakes to find Villa's *Division del Norte* robbing the train she is
on, but before anyone is shot, the American director who is shooting the
scene calls, *Cut!* When she arrives in Houston to go through customs, her
suitcase has not joined her. Maybe it decided to stay in Mexico City and
return to the *Monumento a la Revolución*. Is it the valise John Reed is
holding in the photograph of his arrival in Chihuahua? Maybe it's the
photo from Moscow, or was it the one from Petrograd?

Prequel to *The Apocrypha*

In the apartment upstairs, a man sorts through the piles of his life, what's to be saved, what's to go, and what's to be decided later.

Across the counter, roaches that spread like coins. On the living room floor, a stain that's shaped like a body. In the bathroom, the shower that drips inconsolably.

At the moment of his decision, consequences gather like mercury rolling across hardwood floors toward the lowest corner.

Near the horizon of possibility, the moment of his certainty disguises itself as the illusion of a catalog of losses where new fossils are discovered.

At the borderline of acceptability, refugees wear his voice in the mirror, look like him over the phone.

During the monumental reruns of history, the public eclipses the personal, a picture on the TV of twins embracing in the sky.

Dweller on the Threshold

after a painting by Jamie Wyeth

No one is home at the seaside cottage when I call. I'd leave a note
but I have no notebook. Silence is its own song. I walk around the
wrap-around porch like it's a book, each corner a turn of the page. I'd
call that beach-grass a clean green against the soap-water gray of the
weathered porch wood. Standing in the shade I hear water, wash, waves.
City grit washes off me like sandy feet under a spigot. A bird calls from
the shore. Plover, gull, tern? I've no guidebook to guide me. The beach
sand's as dull as the dun of linen or buckram on a book cover. My hand
covers my eyes as I turn toward the ocean. In the distance I see a boat
with sails of white paper. The craft rises on the waves like a note on a
page of sheet music. I'd trade my calling for a song if I could cover the
payments to make this home my house.

Song of the Servant

Privilegia, with its growing multinational population, is a gated archipelago of enclaves and intrigues that sells out to impresarios and the nouveau-faux when the prices skyrocket over the skyscrapers and investments fever and falter. We nanny their children, give them warm towels, refresh their designer drinks, deliver desserts decorated like Impressionist art, and yield as they ready themselves to descend the grand staircase. As their backs turn from us, our hands slam together like suicidal birds, the applause landing like broken promises on their shoulders, the wing-thrum like thunder ahead of a coming storm.

House on Fire

Twice the building shook. I heard glass rattle before it leaped to
the sidewalks and parking lots below. If the daily newspapers weren't
on strike that week, it would have been deadly for the paperkids. Later,
I heard that all the religious fanatics city-wide disappeared into cracks
which opened below their feet. Holy hell, what irony! Though I
remember how the bed jumped, how it stressed my spine, I'm unsure
even now if it was orgasm or aftershocks. The next day the carpet had
seams slipped, the kitchen was tilted plate stacks and a jumble of pans,
and one whole cupboard was a mosaic of stale cornflakes. Late that
evening a few small fires were still burning. Broken glass in the
alleyways, reflecting the light, could have been cat's eyes. But long
slow kisses could explain that, desire being akin to tongues on fire.

The Connection between Roman Numerals and Letters

after a print by Wendy Collin Sorin

Chromosomes pair like train tracks, tire ruts, ski trails, four-lane
highways; like feet, ears, eyes, wings. The windows to a deaf man's
soul are hands.

One tongue, one palate, one mouth to utter, convey, express, proclaim;
though our hands and eyes betray us. Meager, the body language of
a skeleton.

A concept has angels' wings; hawks' wings that soar above mere words;
shape skating over speaker and listener. Hand puppets are gray gestures
on the wall.

Our pockets filled with our emptinesses and hands, we can no more
carry an idea than a ghost can make a shadow. No wonder I dream of
lost twins.

After the Lighthouse Burns

Beyond beacons, what is dark beyond the border beckons. Boat lantern
by night, candled by distance.

Even illumination, the gleam is clear from afar. Seen from sidewalk and
cul-de-sac and side street, it is no eye.

A fish jumps, spark against tinder.

Under the moon-lens, light bends by a fish-prism, light like flotsam
sparkles ashore. Or just sinks waterlogged.

Nets get cast lightly, spill filaments into lakes, find and fold in fish.

The linoleum moonlight splinters as fish fly by, net raised, the water's
keepsake. See how each scale gleams like a diamond, like an eye.

Until prow points, puts in, is pier tied. Boat lantern wick retracts,
gets extinguished.

But the lightning bugs. Still the stars.

Broken House

We have lived on shores, Pablo, I in my childhood, you in your old
age. Your father traveled on the railroad, mine on the highway. Are we
twins, each of us a Telemachus, astonished as seagulls at the edge of
land and legend?

Tell me, Pablo, why our governments quarrel with our consciences,
each of us in an America where the few feast off the broken, breaking
many. Rock, you say? The sandstone song of the cracked lintel? I see
rock in fields gone to weed, in streets of cities collapsing into rubble.
Holding a stone in my hand, I think of glass.

Come near, Pablo, whisper in my ear. Tell me how you kept your
windows open after finding the back door barricaded by soldiers, the
front door and your trust kicked in. Words are our weapons, colorful
answers that echo after the gun's black question.

Eugene Debs Comes to Canton, Ohio, 1918

The twelve hundred industrial workers standing in the patch of light
under oak and basswood trees here in Nimisilla Park look like foresters,
peasants, serfs. How birth indentures us in this world, how only death
grants us freedom. In between, greed's leeches feed and bloat, leaving
the masses thin as bone soup.

After I finish speaking, these police will close around me like a fist, and
I'll be arrested for the seditious act of speaking the truth. But this won't
finish me. It's but a pause, a disruption like a silence in a conversation
when formulating the next question.

The workers should have this podium, not me. They are tinder and
firewood. My words will be like gasoline, my passion will be the
wind that fans the flames of their revolt. How I want to make them
understand that if they rub together any two of the nothings they own,
the friction will be their own spark. Yes, that is what we need: fire and
water to run the steam engine of social change.

Though I want these laborers to combust, I can't stop picturing this
gentle Nimisilla Creek flowing through the park. If only I could hold
its image in my mind, then put it into theirs, show them that after the
fire, we need water. Isn't that why we flame and rail, why we engage in
struggle — so that we can sit together on the banks of the creek, sisters
and brothers, equal and free, breaking bread instead of heads together?

The ruling class and their bourgeois lackeys believe we desire a
war — we do, but we want a class war. They think we covet their
possessions, the stuff that adds up to the material pile by which they
measure their lives. What we really want is to live in peaceful shade, our
daily lives easy and slow as a creek. But first a speech to fire the boiler.
Then we'll build the factory to forge the world anew.

Dear Beautiful Revolution

after Henri Michaux

Dear government, dear protector, dear big brother: sit down, take off your coat, loosen your tie. Perhaps we can enjoy a cold beer together. Breathe out, dear bureaucratic friend. There. Have some peanuts, a new DVD, a manifesto, these poems.

Relax, you don't have to shave or get saved at church on Sunday. You don't even have to play golf, pretending you enjoy it. Maybe this time you'll sleep through the night. Close your eyes and enter the greenery of our dreams.

We'll be your red convertible, your steak dinner. Your covetousness and unstoppable addictions. See, we're your city in need of paint, your farm buried under blacktop, your territorial suburbs. We're the investment you could call *friend*. In our country, we're the capital.

acknowledgments

I am grateful to the editors of the following journals or anthologies in which these poems, some under different titles or in different versions, first appeared.

Artful Dodge: "You Know What They Say about Pears"
Barn Owl Review: "Blue House" and "Refugees," first published as "The Blue House" and "The Refugees"
Bottle of Smoke: "Schism"
CrossConnect: "Street, City, State, Zip"
Diagram: "Speechless," first published as "Brochure for the Sacred City"
Jenny: "Song of the Servant"
key satch(el): "House on Fire" first published as "Fault Lines"
LIT: "Shadow"
Moonlit: "Extreme Junction" and "Birth of the Cool," first published as "Extreme (J)unction" and "Number 5" respectively
MUSE: "Uninhabited World"
Ocho: "Red House," first published as "What Speech Is"
Ordinary Review: "Greed"
Pleiades: "The Disappeared," first published as "Milk Cartons of the Future"
Poetic Image: "A System of Familiar Philosophy," "Itinerary," and "The Connection between Roman Numerals and Letters." "Itinerary," first published as "Calculating Machine"
Potion: "Rock the Boat"
Potomac: "The John Reed Book Club" and "Late Capitalism"
Riversedge: "Prequel to *The Apocrypha*"
Rougarou: "Café la Habana, Mexico City"
Sentence: "How to Draw a Horse"
Sleeping Fish: "Black House," first published as "Playing the Role of You"
The Prose Poem Project: "In the Orchard, 1891"
Vincent Brothers Review: "Bones," first published as "Strays"

Some of these poems originally appeared in the following chapbooks:

A Box of Light (Columbus, OH: Pudding House)
Against the Simple (OH: Kent State University Press)
Canyons of Sleep (Philadelphia, PA: Plan B Press)
Fellow Traveler (Columbus, OH: Pudding House)
Rock the Boat (White Marsh, VA: All Nations Press)
The Seamless Serial Hour (Columbus, OH: Pudding House)

author biography

Robert Miltner, author of the prize-winning collection of prose poetry, *Hotel Utopia*, was born in Cleveland, Ohio. Miltner holds a doctoral degree in English from Kent State University and is an associate professor of English at Kent State. Since 2006 he has also been a faculty member of the Northeast Ohio MFA in creative writing. He is a three-time Pushcart Prize nominee and winner of the Wick Poetry Chapbook Award for his collection, *Against the Simple*.